# SUPER SLEUTH INVESTIGATORS

## IN

# SECRET OF THE FIRM FOUNDATIONS

BY
CHRISTOPHER P. N. MASELLI

Carson-Dellosa Christian Publishing
Greensboro, North Carolina

# CREDITS

It is the mission of Carson-Dellosa Christian Publishing to create the highest-quality Scripture-based children's products that teach the Word of God, share His love and goodness, assist in faith development, and glorify His Son, Jesus Christ.

*". . . teach me your ways so I may know you. . . ."*
Exodus 33:13

*For Elliana, my daughter,*
*whom I pray will become a woman with firm foundations.*

Author .........................................Christopher P. N. Maselli
Editor .........................................Sabena Maiden
Layout Design ...........................Mark Conrad
Illustrator....................................Stefano Giorgi
Cover Design and Illustration......Nick Greenwood

# TABLE OF CONTENTS

# CONFIDENTIAL INFORMATION

## FOR YOUR EYES ONLY!

Greetings, Super Sleuth! You're about to embark on a series of great adventures as you solve mysteries with me and Nova. We're best friends and business partners with equal stakes in Super Sleuth Investigations, Inc. By "equal stakes," I mean we both came up with the idea of solving mysteries together for fun. And, we're good at it. You can be, too!

This book is packed with twelve mind-bending mysteries that will challenge you to find clues and unravel the answer for yourself. The best part is, at the same time, you'll discover the mysteries of the Bible, too, because Nova and I believe God's Word holds the solutions to all of life's problems.

In this installment, we're going to dive right into the foundations of our faith. We'll look at everything from the meanings of salvation and faith to Jesus' wonderful return. Standing strong as a Christian means having a sure foundation in what you believe . . . and that's what we are going to discover together!

## GET "IN THE KNOW"

OK, so this book is important . . . but it's also fun because you can use it in so many ways! If you've never read one of our mystery books, allow me to show you how it works.

If you're a kid, you can buzz through this just like any other book, reading the mysteries one after another for a good time. Oh wait! There's a neat twist: we don't come right out and tell you the solution to the mystery once we've solved it—we give you the chance to sleuth it yourself! So once you've gathered the clues and think you know the answer, you can read the solution to see if you're right.

If you're a teacher or Sunday school instructor, you'll love the fact that each *Sleuth-It-Yourself* book contains 12 mysteries. So, if you do one a week, you'll have enough for a full quarter. You may decide to hand out copies of the mysteries and read them aloud with the class so that students can look for clues as they go. If no one can solve the mystery, you can go over the story again, stressing key clues until everyone's on the same page. See page 48 for ways to create your own case files.

But, the fun doesn't end there! After each mystery, there is a section called *Under Investigation*. This is like a personal spy journal for writing down ways you can put the Biblical truth you discovered into practice. We've also included a *Word Inspector*, which provides a related Bible verse to memorize. And at the end, you'll find a tough activity to crack. It's plenty of fun for everyone. So, get ready . . . and start sleuthing!

# A DISGRUNTLED CHEF

**"S**o, you're the Super Sleuth Investigators?" asked Steven Taylor skeptically.

Mick Gumshoe nodded. "That's right," he said with a smile. He pointed his thumb at his friend Nova Shrewd who was standing beside him. "I'm Mick and this is Nova. At your service!"

"We may be only thirteen-years-old," Nova said to the man, "but we run a very successful private investigation business."

Mr. Taylor tightened his lips. "Well . . . I suppose the price is fair enough. Your services are free, correct?"

Mick nodded. "Yep, we do this for fun."

"And sometimes cookies," Nova added, "as long as they're made with plenty of chocolate."

"Well," Mr. Taylor said proudly, "I'm the manager of this restaurant—Yums Infinity—and we have this town's most successful lunch buffet." He held out his hand, and Mick and Nova surveyed the dining area. As it was late afternoon, it was largely empty. Still, a waitress scurried about, and several customers were enjoying some snacks. The room smelled of bread and spices. Mick could feel himself getting hungry.

"It's nice," Nova observed.

"Could be better," the manager said. "One thing that holds this place together is that the food is prepared by my great chef. He's one of the best chefs in town. The problem is, I walked into the kitchen this morning and saw him crying. He is obviously disgruntled, and I don't want to lose him. If he were to go to work for Luigi's, it would quickly put me out of business."

"Have you talked to him?" Mick asked. "You know, things aren't always what they seem."

"Things are always what they seem," the manager said. "That's the first rule of business. But, no, I haven't talked to him. That's why I called you. I want you to question him secretly and see if you can figure out why he's ready to leave."

The manager sat Mick and Nova down at a table and ordered them the daily specials: onion soup, roast beef and cheddar sandwiches, and key lime pie. Once they were down to the pie, they asked to speak to the chef. A moment later, a young man dressed in white approached their table.

"This food is wonderful!" Mick said to the chef. "We just had to tell you!"

The chef said, "Thanks. That's always good to hear."

"Yeah, the food was great" said Nova. "Have you worked here long?"

The chef nodded. "Five years."

"So, you enjoy working here then?" Mick asked.

"Mr. Taylor has been very good to me," the chef said. "He lets me decide the menu items and use the freshest ingredients to make them from scratch."

Nova asked, "You make all of the food by yourself?"

"I choose to make the daily specials alone each morning before my staff arrives, but once they're here, I put them to work on the other items."

"You have a good staff?" Mick asked.

"Sure do," the chef said proudly. "We try to satisfy everyone's appetites."

"Hmm," Nova said. "If everything's good here, you must not have any troubles— unless something's wrong at home."

"Things are good there, too," he said. "No complaints."

Mick and Nova thanked the chef for the meal and conversation, and he went back to the kitchen.

A minute later, Mr. Taylor appeared. "Well?" he asked.

"Things aren't always what they seem," Mick said to the manager. "That's the first rule of investigating. Even 2,000 years ago, when Jesus died for us, they thought He was dead for good . . . but things weren't what they seemed. He rose from the dead so that He could save us from death. No one expected that, but it was the truth, and it's one of the firm foundations of our faith."

"So, what's the truth about my chef?" asked the manager.

*Why was the chef was crying?*

*What was the clue?*

*Read the solution to find out!*

SOLUTION

"The truth is," said Mick, "your chef isn't disgruntled at all. In fact, he loves it here!"

"Then, why was he crying?" Mr. Taylor demanded.

Nova tapped her spoon on a bowl in front of her. "If I had to guess, he was crying because he was making the onion soup from scratch all by himself this morning . . . and onions make your eyes water."

The manager chuckled. "That's it?" he shouted. "Onion soup?"

"That's it," Mick said.

The manager smiled. "Then, I certainly owe you all more than just lunch . . . I owe you some chocolate cookies, too!"

---

## Under Investigation

Why did God raise Jesus from the dead?

What does the Bible mean when it says that God "glorified" Jesus?

How will you put your faith and hope in God this week?

*Through him you believe in God, who raised him from the dead and glorified him, and so your faith and hope are in God.*
**1 Peter 1:21**

## Things Are Not What They Seem!

This may look like a picture of just Mick and Nova,
but look closer and you'll see several hidden objects. Can you find all 10?

# WHO STOLE SECOND?

Mick bent down and brushed his hand over the dirt of the infield. It was soft, dusty, and smooth. "This is where second base was?" Mick asked.

"That's it," said Mr. Kent, coach of the Peewees, a local Little League baseball team.

Nova crouched and surveyed the ground. She pointed at some markings in the dirt: a long oval shape and a smaller circle next to one end. "This mean anything?" she asked Mick.

Mick shook his head. "Maybe a footprint . . . hard to tell . . . but it could have been put here anytime."

"The field was graded last night," said the coach. "So, that's a fresh mark."

"If only solving mysteries were as easy as finding the matching shoe," said Mick. "I think this one's going to take talking to some people."

"Well," Coach Kent said, "our team is in the locker room. Once I realized that someone had stolen all the bases, I made sure no one stepped onto the field."

Nova asked, "Why would someone steal the bases?"

"My guess," said the coach, "is that they wanted to stop practice today."

"But why?" Nova pressed.

The coach shrugged.

A few moments later, Mick, Nova, and Coach Kent were standing in front of the Little Leaguers. They were all dressed and ready to go.

A man in a cowboy hat and boots welcomed Mick and Nova. "I'm Roy, the assistant coach," he said. Between gum chews, he shook Mick and Nova's hands.

"Roy's a good friend of mine," said Coach Kent. "His son is Timmy." He pointed to a boy wearing number 14. Timmy waved.

Mick asked, "You get to play much, Timmy?"

"Much as anyone," Timmy responded. "Maybe more."

Nova asked, "Anyone not like playing baseball?"

Number 52 held up his hand. "I don' like it. Mom makes me play 'cuz I got extra rolls." He pulled up his shirt, revealing a pudgy belly.

Roy playfully shielded his eyes. "No one wants to see your belly, boy," he said. Everyone laughed.

Mick asked, "Is there anyone who wants to play a different position?"

Numbers 6 and 39 raised their hands. Nova pointed to Number 6. He said, "I want to play first, but coach has me on outfield. I don't like outfield much."

"Why haven't you told me that, Jeremy?" asked the coach. Number 6 shrugged.

Number 39 spoke up next. "I like playing third base all right, but I'd like to play first once in a while."

Coach Kent nodded.

Mick said, "Look, if one of you stole the bases, this is your chance to tell the truth. We've all done wrong stuff. The Bible says everyone has sinned and fallen short of God's glory. But today, we're giving you a chance to confess."

No one said a word. So, Mick tried a different strategy. "Everyone put out your hands," he said. The boys did as they were told. Mick and Nova looked at them one by one, but none were very dirty . . . not like someone who had just stolen all the bases.

"You have any ideas yet?" Roy asked. "This has me nervous. If we can't practice, we can't win. We don't win, the coach gets replaced, and this team'll be nothing without Coach Kent."

"It'd be fine," Coach Kent said. "You could take over."

"Not without bases!" Roy said strongly.

"There's no need to get upset," said Mick. "I think we've gathered enough clues from our time here."

"You know who stole the bases?" asked Coach Kent and Roy at the same time.

"They don't call us the best sleuths on the supermarket bulletin board for nothing," said Mick.

Who stole the bases?

What was the clue?

*Read the solution to find out!*

## SOLUTION

"The answer," said Mick, "is that the bases were stolen by someone this team trusts."

Nova didn't hesitate. "Roy."

Roy stepped back. "What?"

"Well," said Mick, "after all our questioning, it was the footprint that brought us to the answer."

Everyone on the team looked at Roy's cowboy boots.

"That's right," said Nova. "Roy's the only one wearing shoes that would leave marks on the field from a separated heel and sole."

"But why?" Coach Kent asked.

Roy looked down. "I guess I wanted to be coach after all," he said sheepishly.

## Under Investigation

What does it mean to "fall short of the glory of God"?

What is sin?

How have you sinned recently?

*. . . for all have sinned and fall short of the glory of God . . .*
**Romans 3:23**

# In the "Big Inning"

Whoops! The bases are all out of order.
Can you figure out which base belongs where using the clues below?

Clue #1: Home plate is not by the base with two footprints on it.

Clue #2: Second base is next to third base.

Clue #3: One of the bases with a footprint on it is first base.

Clue #4: The base with the handprint is next to second base.

Clue #5: The plain base is home plate.

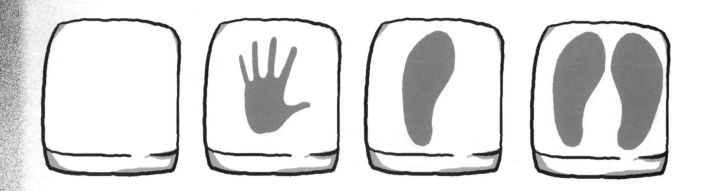

# LOCKED OUT

Rock Johanson, the school's star soccer player, pulled his convertible into the closest parking space and pulled the key out of the ignition. He looked over at Mick Gumshoe sitting beside him and flashed a smile. "Here we are," he said. "My new apartment."

"I can't believe you got your own apartment," Mick said.

"The fast-food business has treated me well," Rock said. He looked into the rearview mirror and raised his eyebrows. "What do you think?"

From the backseat, Nova peered out the window. "It looks pretty nice," she said.

Rock tapped his key on the dashboard. "That's what I said," he replied.

"It's important for me to know you guys like it . . . because I want you to see I've turned over a new leaf. I'm a different person. I'm responsible now."

Mick looked back at Nova. Nova looked forward at Mick. Their expressions showed they shared a common thought: We'll believe it when we see it! The two investigators had solved cases involving Rock before . . . sometimes they had helped him . . . and sometimes they had found him guilty.

The three exited the car. Mick pushed his seat forward and held his door open so that Nova could squeeze out from the back. Once the doors were closed, Rock pressed a button on his key ring, and both doors locked with a simple beep. He led them up a flight of stairs to apartment 3A.

When he reached the door, Rock stood back and said, "Here it is!" He turned the knob and pushed. The door didn't budge. He frowned. Then, Rock put his key in the doorknob. It slid halfway in and stopped. "Oh no," he said.

Mick asked, "What?"

"My key doesn't work," Rock replied. "I knew it!"

"You knew what?" Nova asked.

"My roommate changed the locks!" Rock cried. "I knew I couldn't trust him!"

Mick wondered, "Was it something you did?"

"Well . . ." Rock thought for a moment. "I haven't paid my half of the deposit for the apartment yet. And, I made a lot of long distance phone calls these past few weeks but haven't paid for those, either. Oh! I spilled coffee on the kitchen floor this morning and didn't clean it up. I had to leave for work."

"Well, you've certainly given your roommate a motive," Mick said. "Do you really think he'd lock you out though?"

"What do you think?" Rock asked, twisting the doorknob, his single key hanging out with the electronic key ring dangling from it.

"That's what it looks like," Nova admitted. "I thought you turned over a new leaf."

Mick cracked, "Maybe the leaf turned over again."

"Very funny," Rock said, scowling. "But, I did!"

"I dunno," Nova said. "If your roommate locked you out, it's because you're not being responsible. When you do something wrong, there are always consequences. That's why God warned us that sin always leads to death. He wants us to stay away from it."

"I'm trying!" Rock countered. "But, when my roommate takes revenge into his own hands, it doesn't make things easy!"

"Calm down," Mick said. "Besides, your roommate isn't locking you out to get revenge."

"What?" Rock said. "How do you know?"

*Why did Mick say that Rock's roommate isn't getting revenge?*

*What was the clue?*

*Read the solution to find out!*

## SOLUTION

"He locked me out!" Rock exclaimed.

"Are you sure about that?" Mick asked.

Rock tried the door again. "We're at the right apartment," Rock said, pointing to the 3A on the door.

"That may be," said Mick, "but that isn't the right key."

Nova's face brightened. "Yeah—you're right. That's the key you were using in the convertible's ignition. I know, because it's the only key on the ring, and that ring is what you used to lock the car's doors."

Rock hit himself on his forehead. "Er . . . oh . . . " He dug into his pocket and pulled out another key. It slid right into the lock and turned. "Heh, c'mon in," he said.

---

### Under Investigation

How does sin lead to death?

What does it mean to have eternal life?

How do you receive God's gift of eternal life?

**Word Inspector**

*For the wages of sin is death, but the gift of God is eternal life in Christ Jesus our Lord.*
**Romans 6:23**

## Apartment Search

Help Mick and Nova find their way through the maze to Rock's apartment.

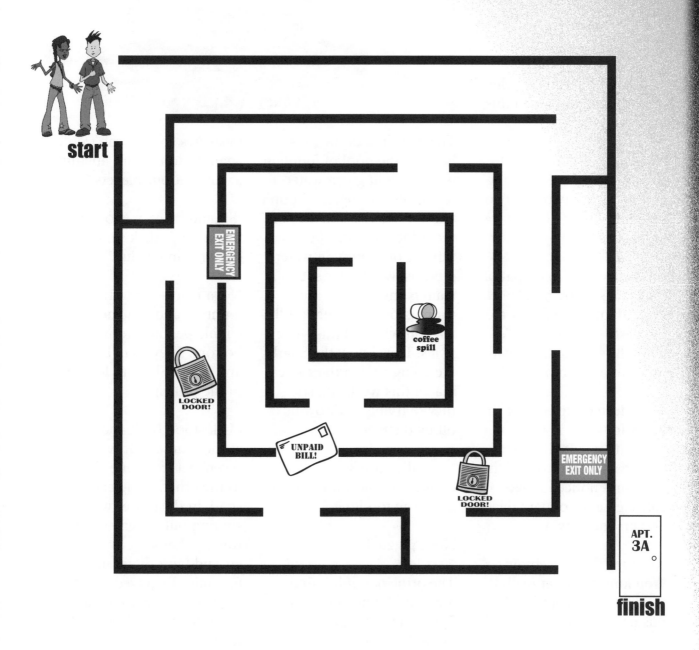

# SEARCHING FOR CLUES

SHARKS DEVOUR!

"Even the smallest clue could be the answer to this one," said Mick.

Nova agreed. "You have to pay attention to everything and try to put two and two together. That's how we stay in business."

Mr. Walker, the principal of the local school, nodded. "Well, I know you guys are the best," he said. "That's why I hired you after I saw this crime this morning."

Mick dusted the edge of the water fountain in front of him with a soft cloth. He looked at the bottom of the cloth and noticed it had collected a lot of dark dust and an ant or two.

Nova raised an eyebrow. "You know, I never really thought of something like this as a crime."

The principal dipped his hand in the pool of fountain water. Bright green water rolled off his fingers. "I don't know what else you'd call it," the principal said. "I think turning our fountain water green is awful. Our soccer team is the Sharks! Blue water is our trademark. I'll tell you who did this—our rivals. They know the Sharks are going to win the soccer match this weekend, so they're trying to throw us off by distracting us."

"Actually," Mick said, "I kind of like the color. It has been blue way too long."

Nova giggled.

The principal didn't find anything humorous. "Just figure out how they did this," he said. "I want to take measures so they can't do it again. I don't want anything to distract our players."

"Should be easy enough to figure out," Mick said, "if we can just find a clue."

Nova reached into the fountain and snatched a couple pennies from the bottom. They were bright and clean. She handed them to the principal.

Mick stood back and looked at the fountain. It was about seven feet from one side to the other. A big cement shark in the center was spitting out water—green water—that shot into the air and back down into the fountain. Engraved across the front of the fountain were the words "SHARKS DEVOUR!"

The principal huffed. "What I can't figure out is how they got rid of our water and replaced it with this. They must have brought in a truck or something."

Mick surveyed the cement around them. "I don't see any evidence of tire tracks," he said.

"Well, however they did it, if I find out exactly who is responsible, I'll make them pay. They'll have no hope."

Nova said, "There's always hope. No matter how bad someone is—they can always find hope in God. He's always there if we call on Him, no matter what

we've done. He'll save even the worst sinner alive."

The principal smirked. "Guess God is more merciful than me."

Mick widened his search. Under some bushes, he found an eraser, a small, yellow bottle cap, and a coupon for Miracle Hair shampoo.

Nova searched on the opposite side of the fountain and found a paper coffee cup and a crumpled math quiz.

The principal looked at his watch. "So . . . you guys close at all to finding out

how this happened?"

"I think we're closer than close," Mick said. "I think I know exactly how they did this."

The principal smiled. "I knew I called the right kids! Do tell!"

*How did someone fill the fountain with green water?*

*What was the clue?*

*Read the solution on page 16 to find out!*

# SOLUTION

"Just as I thought, the smallest clue led me to the answer," said Mick. "Here it is." He held up the small, yellow bottle cap.

"What's that?" asked the principal.

"If I had to guess," said Mick, "I'd say it's the cap to a bottle of yellow food coloring."

"So, that's how they did it!" Nova exclaimed. "They didn't replace the blue water at all. They just added yellow food coloring to it."

"Exactly," Mick said. "Because together, yellow and blue . . ."

"Make green," said the principal. "Brilliant!"

## Under Investigation

What does the Bible mean when it says everyone who calls on the Lord will be saved?

What does it mean to be saved?

When was a time you called on the name of the Lord?

*"Everyone who calls on the name of the Lord will be saved."*
Romans 10:13

## Colorful Crime Stopper

Who could take a really big bite out of crime?
Complete this color-by-number picture and find out!
Be sure to use the same color for each numbered shape.

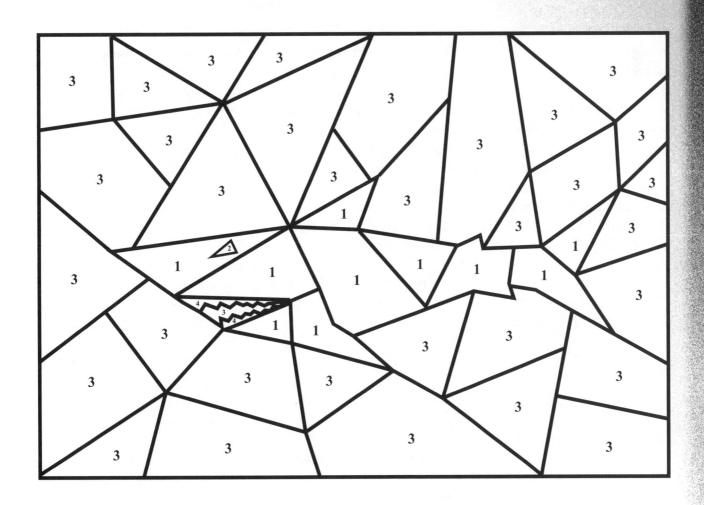

# TOTALLY LOST

"Did you hear something?" Nova asked Mick as they walked down the sidewalk on Thursday morning toward their school bus stop.

"I can't see a thing with the sun in my eyes," Mick said.

Nova tapped Mick on the arm. "I didn't ask you if you saw something, I asked you if you heard something! Are you paying attention, Super Sleuth?"

"It's too early to do that," Mick said with a yawn.

Nova stopped. "There!"

Mick stopped. "What?"

"Someone's crying, I think."

Mick listened. "You're right," he said. He started walking again. "Think it's that kid walking in front of us?"

A few yards ahead of them, a boy was shuffling along.

"Let's see," said Nova. She and Mick picked up their pace until they caught up with the boy. When they reached him, they confirmed Nova's suspicions—he was whimpering, and his eyes were wet.

Mick asked, "You all right, buddy?"

The boy stopped. Mick and Nova stopped.

The boy said, "I can't find my friend!"

"What does he look like?" Mick asked.

"He's a boy," said the boy.

Nova smiled to herself.

Mick said, "Can you be more descriptive?"

"He has a nose," the boy said.

Mick felt a strange sense of déjà vu. "OK, but I'm not sure if we can help you if we don't know more."

"I'm so lost!" the boy exclaimed. "I was supposed to meet him right here, but he's not right here!"

"Where is here?" Nova asked, looking around. "In the middle of this sidewalk?"

"No," the boy said. "Here. He said go north from my house until I got to Salmon Street, and then, turn left. He said to keep walking until I found him."

"Well, maybe you need to keep walking?" Mick suggested.

The boy shook his head. "I don't think so. I've been walking. I've walked four blocks now. He's nowhere around here. I can't find him! I probably passed him. Sometimes, I think I'm so bad at directions that I could even walk past God without seeing Him!"

Nova smiled, "Oh, you couldn't do that. God's everywhere. And to find Him, all you have to do is say that Jesus is your Lord and believe that God raised Him from the dead. You do that, and you'll find Him no matter where you are."

"But, where am I?" the boy shouted.

"Right now," said Nova, "you're in the middle of a sidewalk on the way to our bus stop."

"But, where is my friend?" the boy asked.

"That's simple," Mick replied. "All you have to do is use your smarts to figure it out."

*Do you know where the boy's friend is?*

*What was the clue?*

*Read the solution to find out!*

## SOLUTION

"Your friend," said Mick, "is in the other direction!"

Nova smiled and said, "Mick's right. If you were heading north and were supposed to turn left, then you would have been heading west. But, you're heading into the morning sun. And, since the sun comes up in the east, you must be walking the wrong direction entirely."

"So, if I just turn around and go the other way, I'll run into my friend?" the boy asked.

"I'm sure of it," said Mick. "Unless he went the wrong direction, too!" Mick smiled.

## Under Investigation

Why is it important to believe God raised Jesus from the dead?

What does it mean to confess with your mouth that "Jesus is Lord"?

When have you told someone that you believe Jesus is Lord?

## Perfect Fit

Correctly fit key words from the Word Inspector verse into the crossword grid.

**confess**   **mouth**   **Jesus**   **Lord**   **believe**   **heart**   **raised**   **dead**   **saved**

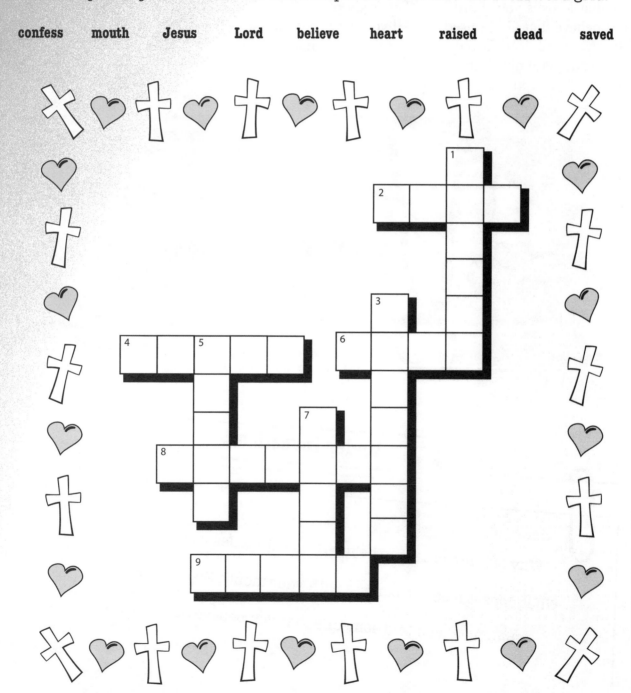

# THE RIGGED CONTEST

"What I need you to figure out," said office manager Jennifer Burger, "is how my assistant is getting the answers to my contests."

"I'm not sure I understand," said Mick, sitting in a plush chair in Ms. Burger's office. Nova sat beside him.

Ms. Burger moved her computer keyboard aside and leaned across her desk. "Every week," she said, "I hold a contest for my office staff. I fill a jar with paper clips and count them as I put them in."

Ms. Burger demonstrated by grabbing a large pickle jar from behind her and placing it in front of the

Super Sleuths. It was jam-packed with paper clips. Thousands of them. "Then," she said, "whoever guesses the number of paper clips inside the jar gets an extra day off that week."

"That's fun," said Nova.

"That's what I thought," said Ms. Burger, "till my assistant got smarter than me."

"How so?" asked Mick.

"She's won the last four times," Ms. Burger said. "By guessing the exact number."

Nova exclaimed, "No way!"

"You would think so," said Ms. Burger, "but that's

exactly what she's done. I can't seem to stump her. Somehow, she's getting the answer, but I just don't know how."

Mick scratched his head. "How do you hide the answer?"

Ms. Burger was already a step ahead of him. She pulled out a notepad. "I write it down on a piece of paper," she said. She wrote a number on the notepad with a pen, then tore the top sheet off. "Now, watch this and tell me if you can figure it out." Next, she folded the paper four times. She pulled out an envelope, slipped the folded paper inside, and sealed the envelope with a lick. Then, she stood up and walked across the room.

Mick and Nova's eyes widened when she pulled at a large painting on the wall and it swung aside, revealing a safe behind it. She punched in some numbers on the safe, and it popped open. She put the envelope inside and closed the safe. It automatically locked. She swung the painting back to its original position and then walked across the room and sat down. "So," she said, "can you guess the number?"

Mick looked at Nova. Nova looked at Mick.

"You sure your assistant doesn't have the code to the safe?" Mick asked.

"Positive," said Ms. Burger. "In fact, I've changed it every week, just in case. There's no way she could break inside."

The three sat silently for a moment. Suddenly, the door opened. Ms. Burger's assistant entered. She was a tall woman with red hair, wearing a dark dress with a pencil tucked behind her ear. "I just wanted to wish you a nice night," she said to Ms. Burger. "I won't see you for a couple days since I have tomorrow off."

Ms. Burger sighed. "You won it fair and square."

A moment later, the assistant left. Ms. Burger sighed. "This is just crazy!"

"Actually," said Nova, "maybe it's what we can't see that's giving her the answer."

Ms. Burger asked, "What do you mean?"

"It's like faith," said Nova. "Faith means believing in things you can't see yet. But, because you believe, they're as good as there."

"So, are you saying she's guessing the number of paper clips in the pickle jar because she believes what others can't?"

"No," Mick said. "What Nova means is that perhaps she's seeing what others are not."

Ms. Burger squinted. "I'm not sure I understand."

"Just watch and see, and things will become more obvious," Mick stated.

*How did the assistant know how many paper clips were in the pickle jar?*

*What was the clue?*

*Read the solution on page 23 to find out!*

## SOLUTION

"This is an old detective trick," said Mick to Ms. Burger. "I got the idea when I saw the pencil your assistant wore behind her ear." He grabbed a pencil and the notepad on which she had written the number. He handed both to Nova. To her he said, "Will you do the honors?"

Nova smiled. "Absolutely!" At once, she lightly shaded the paper with the side of the pencil tip, revealing an impression of a number: 4,784.

"That's amazing!" said Ms. Burger.

"That's seeing what others can't," said Mick. "And, I'm guessing that's what your assistant is doing. So next time, just put your notepad in your safe, too!"

## Under Investigation

What is faith?

How do you show that you have faith?

What is something you're hoping for?

*Now faith is being sure of what we hope for*
*and certain of what we do not see.*
**Hebrews 11:1**

## Count 'Em!

There are a lot of paper clips on this page! How many did you count? _____

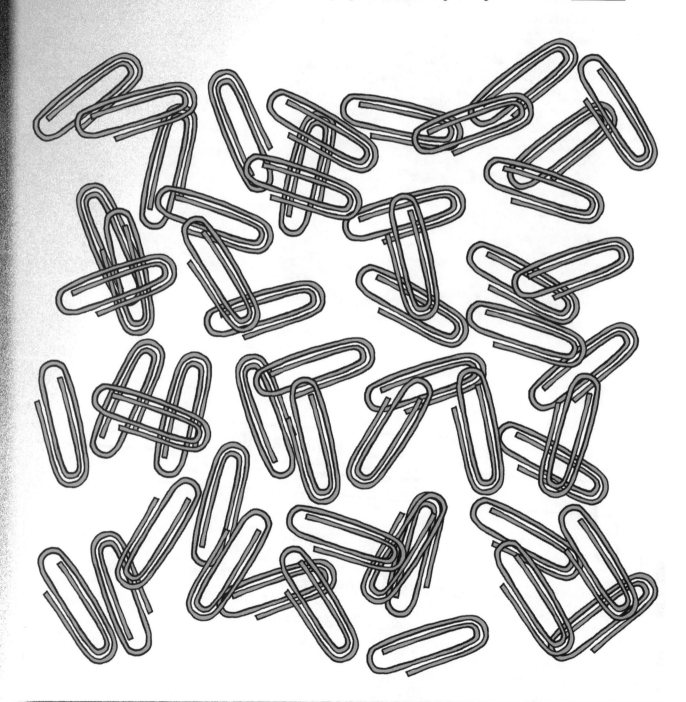

# CAT CHAOS

"You kids have got to help me out now, please!" Miss Trixie exclaimed to Mick and Nova.

Standing on her doorstep, the investigators exchanged glances. Mick said, "That's why we're here, Miss Trixie. How can we help you?"

"My kitty!" Miss Trixie exclaimed. "She's been a very bad kitty!"

Miss Trixie stood aside and let Mick and Nova into her house. They both stopped when they stepped into her living room and saw yarn—everywhere. Around her TV set, draped over her couch, wound around her lamps, tucked around the legs of her chairs . . . literally everywhere.

"This place looks like a tornado came through it," Nova said plainly.

"Tell me about it!" said Miss Trixie. She grabbed a piece of indigo yarn in her hair. "You've got to help me clean up because I'm in trouble!"

"Trouble?" asked Mick. "How's that?" He reached down and picked up a strand of red yarn.

"I was getting ready to knit seven solid-colored hats," Miss Trixie said "one from each color of the rainbow. This morning I left to buy a newspaper at the grocery store. When I returned, I found this!"

"Wait a second," Nova said. "Are you telling us your cat unwound all your yarn in a matter of 15 minutes?"

Nova unwrapped a green strand and a blue strand from a nearby chair leg.

"Yes!" Miss Trixie exclaimed. "When I got home, my kitty had unwound every skein of yarn and wrapped the strings around the room."

Pulling a yellow strand off the lamp, Mick said, "That's crazy!"

Miss Trixie said, "Welcome to my world. The worst part is, I was knitting these hats because I wanted to give them away. I know God likes that sort of stuff, and I figured it would help get me closer to heaven. But now my kitty has ruined all that, and I'm in trouble!"

Nova laughed. "Miss Trixie," she said, "God loves it that you want to give things away, but we don't get to heaven by doing stuff, no matter how good it is. The only way to heaven is by faith—by believing that God exists and that Jesus is His Son who died and rose again for you."

Miss Trixie pulled an orange strand from under a couch cushion and then stopped to rub her chin. "Really? So, my kitty can't keep me out of heaven?"

"Absolutely not!" Mick exclaimed. "You don't really believe that do you?"

"Well . . . of course not!" Miss Trixie stammered. "Still . . . I told my church that I'd have seven hats knit for them in time for our Mission Sunday. But I can only find five colors of yarn here. I'm missing one."

"What happened to it?" Mick asked. He unwound a blue strand from around the television cable box.

"I think she ate it," Miss Trixie said. "And, I don't have time to wait for a hair ball to see what color it was."

Nova stopped pulling at a red strand and winced. "That's a visual I'll have a hard time shaking," she said.

After another half hour of unwinding strands of yarn from around the room and winding them into balls, Mick said, "Well, this one's easy enough. I know exactly what color you're missing."

"You do?" asked Miss Trixie. "What is it?"

*What is the color of the missing yarn?*

*What was the clue?*

*Read the solution on page 27 to find out!*

"Well," said Nova, "you said you were going to make seven hats, one from each color of the rainbow. The colors of the rainbow are red, orange, yellow, green, blue, indigo, and violet. And violet is the only color we haven't uncovered."

Miss Trixie exclaimed, "So that must be what's inside my cat!" Mick and Nova winced.

"Yeah," Mick said. "But rather than wait, I recommend just buying some new yarn."

"Please!" Nova said with a shudder.

## Under Investigation

What are some things people do to try to earn their way into heaven?

Why can't someone get to heaven just by doing good stuff?

What is the biggest gift God has given you?

*For it is by grace you have been saved, through faith—*
*and this not from yourselves, it is the gift of God—*
*not by works, so that no one can boast.*
**Ephesians 2:8–9**

# Code Breaker

What pleases God? Crack the code below to find out!

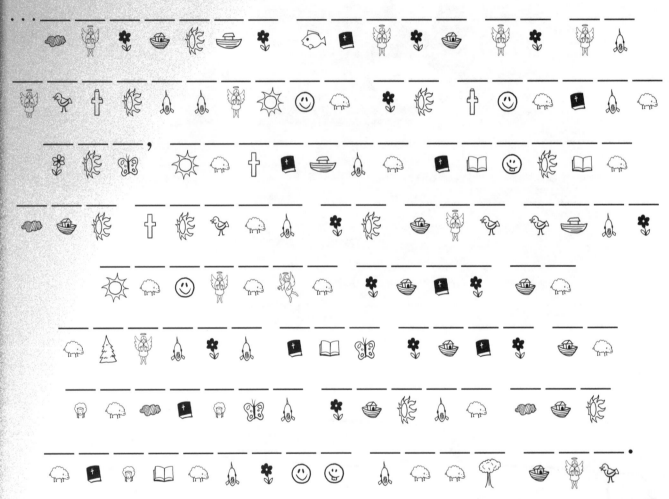

**Hebrews 11:6**

Key:

| A | B | C | D | E | F | G | H | I | J | K | L | M |
|---|---|---|---|---|---|---|---|---|---|---|---|---|

| N | O | P | Q | R | S | T | U | V | W | X | Y | Z |
|---|---|---|---|---|---|---|---|---|---|---|---|---|

# THE VANISHING SCHOOLWORK

A baby-sitter for whom Mick and Nova regularly solved mysteries gave them a frantic phone call one Saturday afternoon. Mick and Nova dropped everything and made their way to the house where she was baby-sitting.

"You do it!" Mick whispered in a hushed voice.

"No, you do it!" Nova whispered back.

"We'll both do it," Mick finally said. At once, both he and Nova knocked on the front door. A moment later, the door swung open. Chuck, a little boy they'd met before, looked at them wide-eyed.

"Hi," Mick said, "is your baby—"

PFFFFFTTTT! Chuck blew a party horn at Mick.

"Oh!" Nova said. "Happy birthday, little guy!"

"It's not his birthday," said the baby-sitter, suddenly approaching the door. "He just believes everything is a constant party. C'mon in."

Mick and Nova stepped inside and saw Chuck tear off through a pile of toys, throwing them around the room. He tossed confetti and laughed like he had just heard the best joke ever. "More cake!" he shouted.

"I think you've had enough sugar!" the baby-sitter shot back. She turned to Mick and Nova, "I don't get paid enough for baby-sitting this kid. He's still learning the meaning of the word 'obey.'"

"So, what can we do for you?" Mick was almost afraid to ask.

"Walk this way," the baby-sitter said. She led them through the kitchen and into the study, complete with a desk, computer, filing cabinet, shredder, small safe, and bookshelf.

At once, Chuck darted into

the study. "Happy birthday!" he mimicked Nova.

Nova smiled. "Cute kid," she said as he shot back out of the room.

The baby-sitter pointed to the desk. "This is where I left my homework," she said. "I was in the kitchen for a minute, and now I can't find my term paper anywhere."

Mick raised his hand. "I bet I know who took it."

"Could it be party boy?" Nova wondered with a gentle smile.

"Without a doubt," said the baby-sitter. "The problem is, I have to find it. It's for my midterm grade. I know he's hidden it around here somewhere."

"We find stuff all the time," Mick said. "Shouldn't be a problem. We can start by talking to Chuck."

The Super Sleuths called him into the study. He didn't come.

The baby-sitter shouted into the hall, "Chuck!" They waited again. Then, she said, "Ugh, why don't little kids understand obedience?!"

"Obedience is something God wants all of us to learn," Nova noted. "He loves it when we obey His commands. Besides, He gave them to us for our own good."

"Well, Chuck better get in here for his own good." Again, the baby-sitter shouted, "Chuck!"

Suddenly, Chuck chugged into the study like a locomotive. "Happy birthday!" he shouted.

Mick asked, "Did you take some papers off this desk?"

A look of surprise hit Chuck's face. Then, he shouted, "Happy birthday!"

"Um, I think he's definitely had too much sugar," said the baby-sitter. "Do you want to start by looking in the living room? It might be under the couch or television set or even outside by now."

"Actually," Nova said, "I hope you saved a copy on your computer. If not, you'd better start typing that term paper again."

"Why is that?" asked the baby-sitter.

*Do you know where the baby-sitter's term paper is?*

*What was the clue?*

*Read the solution on page 31 to find out!*

# SOLUTION

"I think," said Nova, "it's everywhere."

A question mark popped onto the baby-sitter's face. "What do you mean?"

"I mean," Nova said, "that when we walked in, Chuck threw confetti everywhere . . . and there's a shredder about five feet from where you left your term paper."

The baby-sitter's face lost its color. "Oh no. You mean . . . ?"

"Happy birthday!" Mick and Nova shouted together, trying to make the baby-sitter smile.

## Under Investigation

How does obeying God's commands show our love for Him?

Where can you find the commands God has given us?

What specific commands from God are you going to obey this week?

# Party Hat Match

Of the 16 party hats below, each one has a match except one.
Which hat does not have a match?

Bonus: Which hat has five matches? _____

# SECRET VACATION

"**Y**ou're not going to believe this," said Jennifer Burger, sitting behind her nice desk, "but I've got more trouble in this office."

Mick smiled. "It keeps us in business," he said. "What's up now?"

"Well," said Ms. Burger, "last week, right before a company four-day winter break, I bought tickets for a vacation package in Cancun. I can't tell you how much I was looking forward to a quick getaway to the beach!"

"Sounds great," Nova admitted, sitting beside Mick. "Did you have fun?"

"No," said Ms. Burger clicking her teeth together. "That's the problem. Right before I left work, I realized my tickets had disappeared. Later that night, after realizing they were lost for good, I called the airlines and the

hotel I was supposed to use, and they said I had already checked in! I don't know how someone did it with today's security, but someone was very clever and impersonated me and took my vacation."

Mick's forehead wrinkled. "Is everyone back in the office?"

"Yes," said Ms. Burger. "Feel free to walk around and do your thing. Ask questions. Observe. But whatever you do, please find out who stole my ticket. We don't need thieves in our company."

"No," said Nova, "you need people who have character. Those are the kind of people God wants, too. That's why

He told us to live holy."

"Exactly," said Ms. Burger.

Moments later, Mick and Nova walked the floor, from one office to another, greeting workers and listening carefully to their conversations.

"I was giving my SUV a tune-up," said a husky man named Hank when Mick and Nova asked about his weekend. "You know how much gas those things use?"

"So, you weren't out of the country?" asked Mick.

Hank laughed. "Nope. Though, I'd have loved to hit the beach, go jet skiing, and play some volleyball."

A few steps later, they met a young, tan woman named Emily. "I got my hair cut last weekend," she said. "It was pretty low-key."

"So, you weren't out of the country?" asked Nova.

"Nope," Emily said. "I don't even like traveling. It's not natural. I like to eat natural food, have a natural tan, and stay in my natural home. Things are more comfortable that way."

"How about you?" Mick asked a middle-aged woman, named Liza. She had a thick accent. "What were you doing this past weekend?"

"I had family in over ze weekend," she said. "We had 14 kids at my house, running everywhere. It was ze craziest zing you ever saw."

Nova asked, "So, you weren't out of the country?"

"Not zis weekend," she said. "Though I do so long to get away. I 'ave been stuck home chazing ze kids for too many weekends."

Mick and Nova interviewed

three more people before Nova stopped in her tracks.

"What?" asked Mick.

"I just realized something," Nova said. "Something we almost overlooked . . . and it proves who took those tickets!"

"What is it?" Mick asked.

*Do you know who stole the tickets?*

*What was the clue?*

*Read the solution on page 35 to find out!*

Nova said, "I believe Emily was the one who stole the tickets."

"Why do you say that?" Mick asked.

"Well," Nova said, "she said she only likes natural things—but, during the winter, the only way to get a natural tan like she has is to go someplace warm."

"Like Cancun!" Mick cheered.

"Exactly."

## Under Investigation

What does it mean to be holy?

Why does God want us to be holy?

How can living holy give you a better life?

*. . . just as he who called you is holy,
so be holy in all you do.*
1 Peter 1:15

## Quality Word Search

Find the nine positive characteristics listed in the border of the puzzle below.
Words can be found up, down, across, and diagonally.

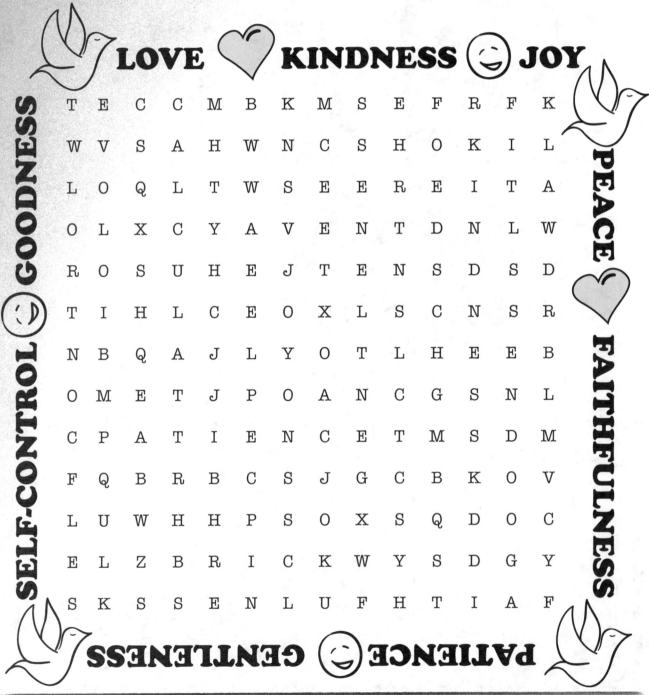

**LOVE** ♡ **KINDNESS** ☺ **JOY**

| | | | | | | | | | | | | |
|---|---|---|---|---|---|---|---|---|---|---|---|---|
| T | E | C | C | M | B | K | M | S | E | F | R | F | K |
| W | V | S | A | H | W | N | C | S | H | O | K | I | L |
| L | O | Q | L | T | W | S | E | E | R | E | I | T | A |
| O | L | X | C | Y | A | V | E | N | T | D | N | L | W |
| R | O | S | U | H | E | J | T | E | N | S | D | S | D |
| T | I | H | L | C | E | O | X | L | S | C | N | S | R |
| N | B | Q | A | J | L | Y | O | T | L | H | E | E | B |
| O | M | E | T | J | P | O | A | N | C | G | S | N | L |
| C | P | A | T | I | E | N | C | E | T | M | S | D | M |
| F | Q | B | R | B | C | S | J | G | C | B | K | O | V |
| L | U | W | H | H | P | S | O | X | S | Q | D | O | C |
| E | L | Z | B | R | I | C | K | W | Y | S | D | G | Y |
| S | K | S | S | E | N | L | U | F | H | T | I | A | F |

**GOODNESS** (left, vertical) · **SELF-CONTROL** ☺ (left, vertical) · **PEACE** (right, vertical) · **FAITHFULNESS** ♡ (right, vertical)

**GENTLENESS** ☺ **PATIENCE** (bottom)

CD-204039 *Secret of the Firm Foundations*

# FRAUD IN THE BALLROOM

"**I** think ballroom dancing is elegant," said Nova.

Mick shook his head. "Not me," he said. "What's elegant about having someone step on your feet?"

"Well," Nova replied, "if you're dancing with someone who is good, she won't be stepping on your feet. I just like it because it seems like an art. It's not easy to learn though."

Mick looked at his watch. "That's why this guy's in business. Now, where is he? He told us he'd meet with us a half hour ago."

"I don't know," Nova replied, tapping her foot. "He probably doesn't want us to meet with him because he knows we might expose the fact that he's a fake."

Mick smiled. "He's innocent until proven guilty," he said.

Nova shook her head. "That's not what Susie told us. She said he charged her $100 and hasn't taught her a thing. She says he doesn't know how to ballroom dance at all."

"We'll see," Mick said.

Ten minutes later, a man emerged from a back room and greeted Mick and Nova with a half-hearted handshake. "What can I do for you?" he asked.

Mick began, "We wanted to check out your studio," he said. "We heard you teach ballroom dancing and wanted to find out more."

"Of course," the man said. "My name is Clyde. I'm the only instructor here, but, when you're as good as I am, who else do you need?"

Mick and Nova exchanged glances.

"And," he said, "I teach here at the best ballroom dancing studio in town. My floor is nearly 1,000 square feet, and I don't charge extra for shoes and tuxedos."

"What do you charge for?" Mick asked.

"Only $100 for four lessons," the man stated. "And, that's practically giving them away. I'm quite generous."

"Can you show us some dances?" Nova asked.

"Um . . . no," the man replied. "I seemed to have hurt my back last week. I'd best not do anything until you actually pay for lessons. Don't need to spin and hurt my back for nothing."

"What dance do you spin in?" Mick asked.

"Many of them!" Clyde said. "That's what makes ballroom dancing so much fun. The fox-trot, waltz, two-step, line dances, swing—you name it. All ballroom dances have spins when you get good."

"You sure sound confident that you know what you're doing," Nova noted.

"Aye," said Clyde, "it's a burden to have so much knowledge. That's why I must share it for only $100 for four lessons. Ballroom

dancing is my passion. It's the only true classical dance."

"I see," said Mick. "Well, we'd better be going. I think we've heard enough."

"What?" Clyde asked. "Don't you like what I want to give to you?"

"Oh, we believe in giving," Nova said. "God said he wants us to give cheerfully— of our time, our money, and our talent. But, we don't believe you should give away something that's worthless."

The man stepped back. "Worthless? My lessons are not worthless!"

"Actually," Mick said, "We're pretty sure they are. And, we have a big clue as to why."

*Why do Mick and Nova believe Clyde is a fraud?*

*What was the clue?*

*Read the solution to find out!*

"We believe your lessons are useless," Mick said, "because you don't even seem to know which dances are ballroom dances and which ones aren't!"

"What?" Clyde exclaimed.

"It's true," said Nova, "Last I heard, line dancing isn't a ballroom dance at all."

"Get out!" Clyde shouted, pointing to the door. But he didn't have to tell Mick and Nova twice. They were already headed that way.

## Under Investigation

Why does God instruct us to give?

What does it mean to give cheerfully?

What is something you can give cheerfully this week?

*Each man should give what he has decided in his heart to give,*
*not reluctantly or under compulsion, for God loves a cheerful giver.*
2 Corinthians 9:7

# Step Up, Step Out

Work your way down through the dance step paths to find the winning dance partner.

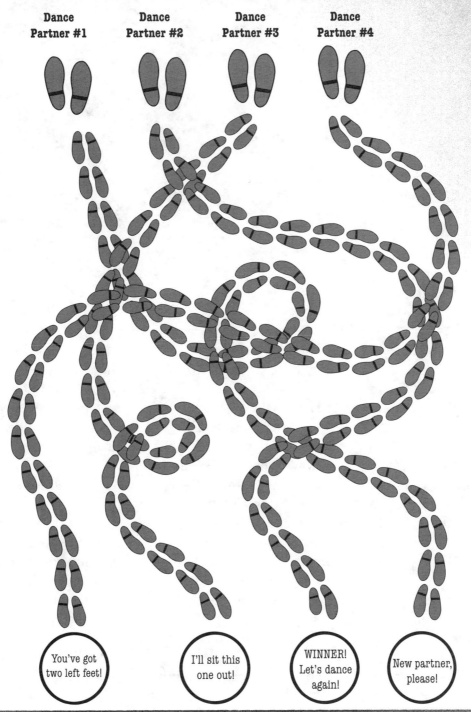

# FREAKY, FOGGY FELLOWSHIP

"This is the place," whispered Sandy Stewart as she led Mick and Nova into the church lobby. She shivered.

"You cold?" Nova asked her. "It's not near as chilly outside today as it has been this past week."

"I'm not cold," Sandy said, pouting. "I'm freaked out." She pushed up her glasses. "This is the place. And, I still don't like it."

"But, it's a church!" Mick replied. "Church is always a wonderful place to come. When you walk in the doors, you can feel the love, the joy, the—"

"Freakiness," Sandy muttered. "I won't come to this church anymore."

"Why not?" Nova asked.

"There doesn't seem to be anything wrong with it."

"That's why I brought you here," said Sandy. "I've heard you say that things aren't always what they seem. I need you to find out why it seems so freaky in here."

"Well . . . what makes it freaky to you?" Mick asked.

"The fog," said Sandy.

"The fog?" questioned Nova.

"The fog," repeated Sandy.

"Last week when I came in here . . . all alone . . . the room was filled with this creepy fog everywhere I looked. I couldn't get away from it."

"Fog? Indoors?" Mick asked.

"Fog. Indoors," Sandy said. "I tried shouting for help, but my voice caught in my throat. So, I just ran back out the church doors and all the way home."

"Was it foggy outside?" Mick questioned.

"Nope, just inside," said Sandy. "I don't want to go to any church that fills up with fog like a dark alley."

"That is kind of freaky," Nova admitted. Mick shot her a glance as if to say, don't encourage her!

Mick grabbed a nearby chair and moved it under a heating vent. He stood on the chair and looked closely at the ceiling. Small black marks peppered the ceiling around the vent. "We'll find the answer," Mick said, "because you can't stop attending church! God wants us to go to church so that we can hear His Word, worship Him, and encourage one another."

"That's all fine and dandy," said Sandy, "but I can't encourage anyone if I can't see them because of the fog."

Mick stepped off the chair and slid it back into place. The impressions of the chair's feet were still on the carpet.

"How long have you been coming here?" Nova asked Sandy.

Sandy shrugged her shoulders. "For as long as I can remember," she said. "Until it freaked me out last week. I haven't been back since."

Nova grabbed a Bible from a table and thumbed through it. The edges were worn from use. She set it back down on the table.

"Is there anything else you can tell us?" Mick wondered. He moved to the nearby doors and opened them. A gust of air flooded the room. He closed the doors, and it soon became warm again.

"I don't think so," Sandy said thoughtfully.

Nova nodded. "That's all right. I think I know how it got foggy in the church lobby," she said.

"You do?" Sandy exclaimed. "Please tell me how!"

*Do you know how the lobby became foggy?*

*What was the clue?*

*Read the solution on page 42 to find out!*

"We should have seen it right away," said Nova. "It has to do with your glasses and how cold it was last week."

"I don't understand," said Sandy.

"Ah!" Mick shouted. "I do! When you came inside, your glasses fogged up from the sudden change of temperature—it was warm in here and cold outside. To you, it appeared as though the entire room fogged up—even though it was just your glasses."

"How creative!" Sandy exclaimed.

Nova added, "And how right!"

## Under Investigation

Why is it important to attend church?

Why do some people stop going to church?

Why is it important to encourage one another?

Word Inspector

*Let us not give up meeting together, as some are in the habit of doing,*
*but let us encourage one another—*
*and all the more as you see the Day approaching.*
Hebrews 10:25

## Foggy Words

Read the following wacky words and write them on the lines below.

1. ENCOURAGE

2. GLASSES

3. N'ck

4. FELLOWSHIP

5. NOVA

6. CHURCH

1. _____

2. _____

3. _____

4. _____

5. _____

6. _____

# MATH ALLERGIES

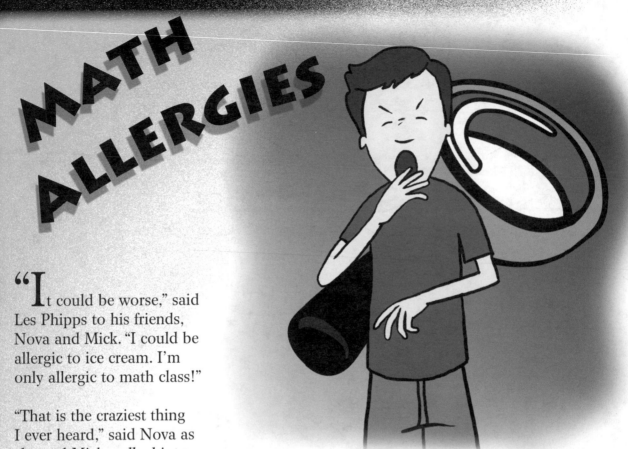

"It could be worse," said Les Phipps to his friends, Nova and Mick. "I could be allergic to ice cream. I'm only allergic to math class!"

"That is the craziest thing I ever heard," said Nova as she and Mick walked into math class with Les. The bell had yet to ring, and students were milling slowly into the classroom.

"You heard me yesterday," said Les. "I sneezed through half the class."

"I thought you were just trying to get out of doing your homework," Mick said with a smile and a playful jab to Les's ribs.

"Well, that would have been nice," Les said. He sat down in the front of the room, across from the teacher's desk. Mick sat behind him. Nova sat beside him.

"Maybe it'll go better today," Mick said hopefully. "Maybe we won't be covering fractions again."

"Very funny!" Les exclaimed. He pulled out his math book and opened it. "But you wouldn't be laughing if it were y-y-ah-ah-ah-chooooo!" He sneezed very loudly.

Mick looked at Nova. Nova looked at Mick.

Mick jumped up and stood in front of Les. "You just sneezed!" he said.

Les closed his math book. "Ah-chooooo!"

Nova pushed her math book off her desk.

"Ah-chooooo!"

Mick turned around and closed the math book on the teacher's desk. He tipped over a jar of pencils and a vase of fresh flowers. An apple rolled across the desk and hit the floor.

"Ah-chooooo!" Les cried. "Jesus needs to come back right now and save me from this! I can't stand it anymore!"

Nova laughed. "Jesus is coming back soon, but only He knows when. That's a hope we have as Christians. He won't leave us!"

Les said, "Well, I hope He comes back quickly! I can't take this sneezing!"

The teacher, Ms. Jacobs, entered the room and picked up her apple. "What's going on here?" she exclaimed.

"I'm allergic to math!" Les cried. "I keep sn-sn-ah-ah-ah-chooooo!"

"This is just crazy!" Mick shouted.

A kid in the back of the room raised his hand. "Can I be allergic to math, too?"

Ms. Jacobs said, "I highly doubt anyone is allergic to math, Jason."

"I am!" said Les. "I might even be allergic to spelling. Maybe homework, too!"

Nova wondered, "Hey Les, do you think you're allergic to P.E.?"

Les stopped sneezing. "I doubt it. Ah-chooooo!"

"How did this start?" asked Ms. Jacobs.

"He opened his math book," said Mick.

"And, I opened my math book," said Nova.

"And, your math book was already open," Les said to the teacher. "Ah-chooooo!"

"I've never heard of this before!" said Ms. Jacobs. "Get yourself to a safe place—go into the hallway!"

Quickly, Les jumped up, nearly tripped over a book bag, and ran out of the classroom with a big, wide grin on his face.

Then, they waited . . . and waited . . . and waited . . . but, they didn't hear him sneeze again.

"Come back in here!" Mick shouted to Les.

Les walked back into the room, still smiling. "Thanks. All better," he said. He took his seat.

Nova opened her math book slowly, watching Les as she did it.

"Ah-chooooo!" Les sneezed extremely loudly.

"What in the world!" cried the teacher. "I just do not understand what is going on here with Les! This does not make any logical sense!"

"Hey, wait a second," said Mick. "You're right, Ms. Jacobs. He cannot be allergic to math. But, there is a reason that Les is having this horrible sneezing reaction."

"Why?" asked Les with a questioning look.

"Yes, why?" asked Ms. Jacobs. "I plan to give you all a quiz tomorrow, and we need an answer to this crazy allergy thing now."

*Why did Mick says that Les isn't allergic to math?*

*What was the clue?*

*Read the solution on page 46 to find out!*

# SOLUTION

"First of all," Mick said, "it's impossible to be allergic to math."

"Ah-chooooo!" sneezed Les. "I beg to differ!"

"I think you're allergic to something else," Mick said.

"Like what?" asked the teacher.

Nova got the clue. "Like the only other thing nearby that would likely cause an allergic response," she said, "are the fresh flowers on Ms. Jacobs' desk."

Ms. Jacobs turned around and grabbed the flowers that had been standing in a vase right in front of Les's desk. She tossed them out the window.

A long moment went by, and Les didn't sneeze.

"Case solved! And a math quiz tomorrow," Mick said.

Les sighed. "I never thought I'd wish a case was still unsolved. I liked my solution better!"

## Under Investigation

When is Jesus coming back to earth?

Why is Jesus coming back?

How can you get ready for Jesus' return?

*He who testifies to these things says,*
*"Yes, I am coming soon." Amen. Come, Lord Jesus.*
**Revelation 22:20**

## Mathematical Possibilities

Using numbers 0–4, correctly fill in the puzzle below. The numbers added across should equal the numbers on the right. The numbers added down should equal the numbers at the bottom. And, the numbers added diagonally should equal the numbers at each end. (Numbers may be repeated.)

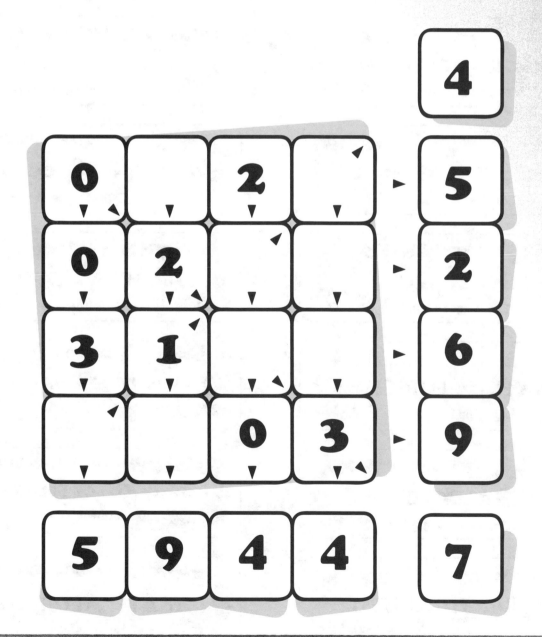

# SUPER SLEUTH CASE FILES

Create case files for your own Super Sleuths to solve during free class time. Make 12 copies of page one of this book, trim the margins, and attach each to the cover of a file folder. Copy the labels below onto extra large ($^{15}/_{16}$" × 3 $^{7}/_{16}$", 2.38 cm × 8.73 cm) file folder labels or simply cut them out and tape them to the file folder tabs. Copy each mystery story once and copy enough corresponding activities for each student. Then, place them in the appropriate folders.

Case #1
## A DISGRUNTLED CHEF
The Resurrection

Case #2
## WHO STOLE SECOND?
All Have Sinned

Case #3
## LOCKED OUT
The Wages of Sin

Case #4
## SEARCHING FOR CLUES
Calling on God

Case #5
## TOTALLY LOST
Making Jesus Your Lord

Case #6
## THE RIGGED CONTEST
What Faith Is

Case #7
## CAT CHAOS
Not Saved By Works

Case #8
## VANISHING SCHOOLWORK
Obedience

Case #9
## SECRET VACATION
Holiness

Case #10
## FRAUD IN THE BALLROOM
Giving Cheerfully

Case #11
## FREAKY, FOGGY FELLOWSHIP
Assembling Together

Case #12
## MATH ALLERGIES
Jesus' Return